The Ukrainian Cookbook

Traditional and Modern Recipes

Marit Peters

Contents

43 - Cutlets (Sichenyky)
44 - Stuffed Cabbage (Holubtsi)
45 - Goose with Apple Stuffing
46 - Buckwheat with Pork (Kasha)
47 - Chicken Kiev (Kotleta po-kyivsky)
48 - Pork Roll with Mushrooms (Kruchenyky)
49 - Meat Patties (Kotlety)
50 - Meat Jelly (Holodets)
51 - Pork and Prunes
54 - Pearl Barley Pudding (Kutia)
55 - Honey Cake (Medovik)
57 - Cottage Cheese Cake (Babka)
58 - Easter Cheese (Paska)
59 - Plum and Cheese Dumplings
61 - Apple Cake (Yabluchnyk)
62 - Strawberry Jam
63 - Cheese Pancakes (Syrniki)
64 - Walnut Stuffed Prunes
65 - Coffee Jelly
66 - Plum Kyselitsa
67 - Uzvar
68 - Spiced Vodka
69 - Kvass

Introduction

Ukrainian cooking has a long tradition. This large country has lots of high quality fertile farming land and a variety of great produce and this has shaped the history of cooking in the area. Ukraine has been under the control of different countries and empires in its history, and this had influenced the cuisine, with similarities to cooking in nations such as Russia, Poland and Austria.

Many dishes have developed from the peasant population, and Ukrainian staple ingredients are rye, wheat and grains, beetroot, potato and cabbage. Meat and fish are naturally very popular also.

The national dish of the Ukraine is borscht. The most famous version of this soup is made from beetroot, but numerous other varieties such as cabbage borscht are made.

Pickled Mushrooms

Ingredients

3 lbs/1.3 kg of button mushrooms with stems removed
13 peppercorns
1 tablespoon of juniper berries
3 quarters of a cup/75g of sugar
3 quarters of a cup/180ml of vinegar
salt

Put the mushrooms in 4 cups/960ml of hot water with 1 tablespoon of salt. Cook on a moderate heat for 10 minutes.

Drain the mushrooms and place in jars.

Put 1 and a half cups/360ml of water in a pan with the peppercorns and juniper berries and bring to the boil, then cook for 30 minutes. Add the 2 tablespoons of salt and the sugar and cook for 7 minutes. Add the vinegar, bring to the boil, then pour the liquid over the mushrooms in the jars. Put a lid on the jars. Place in the refrigerator for 2 days.

Dill Sauce

Ingredients

1 tablespoon of chopped dill
2 tablespoons of butter
2 tablespoons of flour
1 cup/240ml of stock
half a cup/120ml of cream
salt
two tablespoons of lemon juice

Put the butter in a pan. Add flour and make a paste. Add the stock and cook and stir for 6 minutes.

Take off the heat. Add the cream, dill, lemon juice and some salt and mix.

Wild Garlic and Cottage Cheese Salad

Ingredients

3 tablespoons of chopped wild garlic
2.1 oz/60g of grated celeriac
7 oz/200g of sweetcorn
2.8 oz/80g of cheese
7 oz/200g of cottage cheese
salt
pepper

Mix the ingredients together in a bowl.

Gooseberry Sauce

Ingredients

1 cup/100g of gooseberries
2 egg yolks
2 tablespoons of butter
1 tablespoon of flour
1 third of a cup/35g of sugar
half a cup/120ml of chicken stock
a quarter of a cup/60ml of sour cream
salt

Put the gooseberries in a saucepan with the butter. Cook for 10 minutes. Add the flour, stock, sugar and some salt. Stir to make a smooth mix. Cook for 8 minutes on a medium heat stirring several times. Add the egg yolks and cream, stir well, and bring to the boil.

Serve the sauce with chicken.

Green Beans with Sour Cream

Ingredients

1 lb/453g of green beans chopped in half
2 chopped tomatoes
1 deseeded and chopped green pepper
1 sliced onion
3 quarters of a cup/180ml of sour cream
3 tablespoons of butter
salt
black pepper

Put the beans in a pan of boiling salted water. Boil for 10 minutes. Drain.

Cook the onion and pepper in the butter in a saucepan over a medium heat for 7 minutes. Add he tomatoes and cook for 4 minutes.

Add the sour cream and some salt and pepper. Mix well. Serve warm.

Vegetable and Caraway Soup

Ingredients

1 cup/340g of cooked chopped vegetables e.g. carrot, beetroot, cabbage
2 tablespoons of caraway seed
flour
4 cups/960ml of stock
butter
salt
pepper

Put the 1 cup/240ml of water in a pan and boil. Add the seeds and cook on a low heat for 10 minutes. Leave for 20 minutes, then drain the seeds, keeping the liquid.

Boil the stock and add the vegetables. Put the flour and butter in a pan and make a paste. Add to the stock. Add the caraway liquid and some salt and pepper. Bring the soup to the boil.

Cucumber Soup

Ingredients

3 peeled and sliced cucumbers
half a cup/170g of chopped spinach
2 chopped spring/green onions
1 tablespoon of chopped dill
1 tablespoon of chives
2 tablespoons of butter
2 tablespoons of flour
half a cup/120ml of cream
4 cups/960ml of stock
salt
pepper

Put the cucumbers, onion and spinach in a pan with the butter. Cook on a low heat for 10 minutes.

Add the flour and some salt and pepper and mix. Add the stock then cook on a low heat for 15 minutes.

Blend the soup and put in the refrigerator for an hour.

Serve cold with dill chives and cream

Cabbage Soup

Ingredients

1 chopped cabbage
1 chopped carrot
2 chopped onions
half a cup/100g of pearl barley
1 bay leaf
1 tablespoon chopped dill
1 tablespoon chopped parsley
6 peppercorns
8 cups/1.9 litres of stock
sour cream

Bring the stock to a boil in a pan. Add the barley, then cook on a low heat for 2 hours.

Add the carrot, cabbage, onion, bay lead, peppercorns parsley and dill. Bring to the boil, then cook on a low heat for 15 minutes - until the carrots and cabbage are cooked.

Serve with some sour cream.

Green Borscht
(Zelenyj borshcht)

Ingredients

2 chopped carrots
2 chopped potatoes
3 cups/90g of chopped sorrel
2 tablespoons of vinegar
3 cups/720ml of water or stock
dill
salt
black pepper
sour cream

Boil the water. Add the potatoes and carrots. Cover and cook on a medium heat for 15 minutes - until cooked.

Add some salt and pepper. Add the sorrel and remove from the heat.

Serve with some sour cream and dill on top.

Cabbage and Apple Soup

Ingredients

1 peeled, cored and chopped green apple
3 cups/267g of chopped red cabbage
1 sliced onion
1 tablespoon of raisins
4 cups/946ml of stock
quarter of a cup/60m of cider vinegar
quarter of a cup/50g of brown sugar
1 tablespoon of apple butter
butter
salt
pepper

Cook the apple and onion in some butter for 8 minutes. Add the cabbage and cook for 6 minutes.

Add the stock and vinegar. Bring to the boil then add the sugar, raisins and some salt and pepper. Cook on a low heat for 1 hour.

Stir in the apple butter.

Pancakes (Nalesniki)

Ingredients

1 cup/110g of flour
2 eggs
1 cup/236ml of milk
half a cup/118ml of carbonated water
salt
3 tablespoons of butter

Mix the ingredients apart from the butter in a bowl to make a batter.

Fry the batter in butter to make the pancakes.

Mushroom Pate

Ingredients

14 oz /400g of a variety of chopped mushrooms
1 chopped onion
half a cup/120g of cream cheese
half a cup/120g of curd or cottage cheese
2 tablespoons of chopped tarragon
12 tablespoons of chopped parsley
butter
salt
pepper

Put the mushrooms and onion in a pan with the butter. Cook for 7 minutes stirring frequently.

Mix the cheese and herbs in a bowl. Add some salt and pepper. Add the mushrooms and onion and mix.

Potato Dumplings
(Pampushki)

Ingredients

3 peeled and grated potatoes
1 mashed potato
half a cup/80g of farmers cheese (or cottage cheese)
fresh chopped chives
1 cup/140g of flour
1 beaten egg
1 cup/125g of dried breadcrumbs
salt
black pepper

Mix the grated and mashed potato in a bowl with some salt
and pepper.

In another bowl mix the cheese, some chives and some salt.

Create small dumpling shapes from the potato. Put some of
the cheese mix in the middle of each dumpling and enclose the
cheese with the potato. Roll the dumplings into balls.

Put the dumplings in the egg, then coat in the breadcrumbs.

Fry in oil for 10 minutes - or until cooked - browning on each
side.

Olivier Salad

Ingredients

5 peeled and chopped boiled potatoes
1 sliced carrot
4 boiled chopped eggs
6 chopped pickles
15 oz/425g of cooked green peas
half a cup/65g of chopped ham
half a cup/115ml of mayonnaise
parsley

Mix the potato, egg, carrot, pickle, parsley, ham and peas in a bowl. Mix in the mayonnaise.

Cabbage Buns (Pyrizhky)

Ingredients

25 oz/700g of sauerkraut
half a chopped onion
3 cups/700ml of water
half a cup/50g of sugar
8 cups/1.1 kg of flour
4 and a half teaspoons of yeast
1 tablespoon of sugar for yeast
2 eggs
1 cup/200ml of vegetable oil
salt
pepper
two tablespoons of butter

Warm the water. Add half a cup to a jug with 1 tablespoon of sugar and the yeast. Leave for 10 minutes.

Mix the eggs, oil, sugar and the rest of the water. Add the yeast mix.

Mix the flour with some salt. Add to the other mixture and stir well to make a dough.

Knead the dough for 10 minutes. Put the dough in plastic wrap and leave for 30 minutes.

Mix the onion and sauerkraut in a blender. Then fry the mix in the butter for 7 minutes. Add some pepper.

Take small squares of the dough. Put spoonful of sauerkraut in on them and enclose it in the dough pieces.

Put on a baking tray on baking paper.

Bake in a preheated oven at 350F/176C for 12 minutes.

Potato and Cheese Varenyky

Ingredients

5 peeled and diced potatoes
1 cup/125g of grated cheese
2 chopped onions
5 cups/700g of flour
2 tablespoons of butter
1 cup/236ml of milk
1 tablespoon of sour cream
half a cup/118ml of water
butter
salt

Mix the flour in a bowl with a teaspoon of salt. Add 2 tablespoons of butter and the milk and sour cream. Make a sticky dough, adding the water.

Put in a bowl then leave for 30 minutes.

Put the potatoes in a pan with enough water to cover. Bring to the boil, then cook for 10 minutes. Drain

Put some butter in a pan and fry the onions for 8 minutes.

Put the onions in a bowl with the cheese and some salt and pepper.

Roll out the dough and cut out cookie shaped circles. Put spoonfuls of potato mix on the dough pieces, then fold in half to cover the mix, and seal the edges. Coat the dough pieces in flour.

Put the dough pieces in a pan of boiling water. Cook for 5 minutes. Put the pieces in a lightly oiled bowl.

Serve with sour cream.

Goose with Apple

Olivier Salad

Vegetable Pottage (Yushka)

Ingredients

1 chopped carrot
3 chopped potatoes
1 egg
2 sliced onions
1 cup/140g of flour
half a cup/120ml of water
2 cups/480ml of stock
3.5 oz/100g of pork fat
salt

Mix the flour, some salt, egg and water together to make a dough.

Roll the dough into a tube shape. Cut into pieces.

Put the potato and carrot into pan with the stock. Bring to the boil and cook for 5 minutes. Add the dough pieces and cook for 20 minutes.

Fry the onions and pork fat for 7 minutes.

Add the onion and fat to the broth.

Porcini in Sour Cream

Ingredients

1.3 lb/600g of chopped porcini mushrooms
7 oz/200g of sour cream
1 chopped onion
1 clove of crushed garlic
salt
black pepper
parsley

Fry the onion in some oil for 6 minutes. Add the mushrooms and cook for 10 minutes. Add salt and pepper.

Add garlic and the sour cream. Cook on a low heat for 10 minutes. Add some chopped parsley.

Bean and Cabbage Soup (Kapusnyak)

Ingredients

4 oz/113g of chopped bacon
1 chopped stick of celery
1 chopped onion
2 chopped carrots
2 peeled and chopped potatoes
16 oz/453g of white beans
2 lbs/900g of sauerkraut
9 cups/2.6 litres of chicken stock
2 cups/480ml of water
oil
salt
pepper

Cook the bacon in the oil for about 6 minutes - until browned.

Remove the bacon from the pan and place on a plate.

Put the onion and celery in the pan and cook for 6 minutes.

Add the potato, carrot and broth, and a cup of water. Bring to the boil. Cook on a low heat for 15 minutes.

Add the sauerkraut, bacon and white beans. Cook on a medium heat for 12 minutes - until the potato is cooked. Add some salt and pepper.

Potato Pancakes (Deruny)

Ingredients

4 grated potatoes
1 egg
3 tablespoons of flour
1 grated onion
sour cream
salt

Mix all the ingredients in a bowl to make a batter. Fry tablespoons of the mix in oil for 5 minutes on each side until browned.

Serve with sour cream.

New Potatoes with Sour Cream

Ingredients

2 lb/907g of new potatoes
2 chopped spring/green onions
4 tablespoons of chopped dill
1 cup/240ml sour cream
salt

Put the potatoes in a pan of hot water, bring to the boil, cover and cook for 25 minutes.

Drain the potatoes and peel them. Put them in a bowl and add the cream and some salt.

Top with the onions and dill.

Mashed Potatoes

Ingredients

3 lb/1.3kg peeled and chopped potatoes
half a cup/120ml of cream
half a cup/120ml of sour cream
10 tablespoons of butter
salt
white pepper

Put the potatoes in a pan. Cover with water and bring to the boil. Then cook on a low heat for 25 minutes - until cooked. Drain a put in a bowl.

Put the butter and cream in a pan. Cook for 3 minutes. Mash the potatoes adding the cream, butter, sour cream and some salt and pepper.

Pike with Horseradish

Ingredients

2 lb/900g of pike cleaned and gutted and cut into pieces
5 tablespoons of grated horseradish root
beaten egg
half a cup/120ml of sour cream
1 teaspoon of sugar
1 tablespoon of fresh dill
dried breadcrumbs
salt
black pepper

Dip the fish in egg, then in the breadcrumbs.

Fry fish in hot oil for 6 minutes, making sure all sides are browned.

Mix the horseradish with the cream, dill, sugar and some salt.

Serve the fish with the sauce.

Potato Pancakes

Potato and Cheese Varenyky

Battered Fish Strips

Ingredients

1 lb/450g of sole fillets cut into strips
1 cup/120g of flour
1.7 oz/50g of cornflour/cornstarch
2 tablespoons of fresh chopped dill
2 teaspoons of salt
lemon juice
oil

Mix the flour, cornflour and salt in a bowl. Add some ice water to make a batter. Leave for 50 minutes.

Mix the sole with the dill. Put some flour in a bowl with some salt and pepper. Coat the fish in this flour. Dip in the batter. Fry in hot oil for 4 minutes.

Fish with Tomato

Ingredients

2 lbs/907g of cod cut into pieces
1 chopped onion
1 chopped carrot
5 oz/141g of tomato puree/paste
2 bay leaves
3 tablespoons of sugar
salt
black pepper
oil

Fry the fish in some oil for 5 minutes.

Remove the fish. Put the onions and carrot in the pan and cook for 5 minutes. Add the tomato, sugar, bay leaves and 4 cups of water. cook on a moderate heat for 6 minutes, stirring frequently.

Add the fish to the pan. Cook on a low heat for 60 minutes.

Fish Cutlet

Ingredients

1.1 lb/500g of ground/minced fish fillet
beaten egg
flour
dried breadcrumbs
butter
black pepper
salt

Mix the fish with some butter and salt and pepper. Make into patty shapes.

Coat in beaten egg, then in the breadcrumbs.

Fry in butter until browned for 6 minutes on each side - until the fish is cooked

Carp in Sour Cream

Ingredients

1 carp
2 lb/907g peeled and chopped potatoes
5 oz/141g chopped bacon
1 chopped onion
half a chopped green bell pepper
2 sliced tomatoes
salt
black pepper
2 tablespoons of melted butter
1 cup/240ml of sour cream
1 tablespoon of flour

Put the potatoes in a pan of boiling water. Cook on a low heat for 20 minutes. Drain. Then slice the potatoes.

Cook the bacon in a pan for 7 minutes.

Put layers of potato, then tomato, pepper, onion and bacon and some salt and pepper in a baking dish.

Cut the skin of the fish in several places. Season with salt. Put in the baking dish. Bake in a preheated oven at 400F/204C for 40 minutes.

Mix the cream, flour and some salt. Pour over the baking tray. Cook for another 20 minutes - until carp is cooked.

Fish with Cheese, Lemon and Mushrooms

Ingredients

10 oz/283g carp cut into fillets
1 chopped onion
3 grated carrots
7 fl oz/200ml of sour cream
8 oz/230g of grated cheese
10 oz/280g of chopped mushrooms
1 sliced lemon
black pepper
salt
fresh chopped dill

Rub the fish with some salt and pepper. Refrigerate the fish for 30 minutes

Fry the carrot and onion in some oil for 10 minutes. Add the mushrooms and cook for 10 minutes.

Put the fish on foil on a baking tray. Put lemon slices on top and the sour cream. Then put on the carrot, mushroom and onion mix. Finish with the cheese. Cook on a preheated medium oven for 50 minutes - until the fish is cooked.

Halibut with Tomato

Ingredients

1 lb/453g of halibut fillets
half a cup/37g of sliced mushrooms
2 chopped onions
1 chopped carrot
half a cup/65g of chopped celeriac
4 peeled and chopped tomatoes
half a cup/120ml of heavy cream
1 tablespoon of capers
salt
black pepper
1 tablespoon of juniper berries

Put the carrots, onion, tomato, 4 and a half cups of water, juniper berries and 2 tablespoons of butter in a pan. Bring to the boil, then cook on a low heat for 30 minutes. Drain the mix into a bowl using a sieve/colander. Put the stock back in the pan and add the fish. Bring to the boil, then simmer for 6 minutes.

Put the fish on a plate.

Bring the stock to the boil and cook for 8 minutes. Add 2 tablespoons of butter to another saucepan. Add the mushrooms and fry for 5 minutes. Add the cream stock and stir in the cream. Add the capers and some salt and pepper. Serve with the fish.

Carp with Buckwheat

Ingredients

1 carp
2.1 oz/60g of dried porcini
1 sliced onion
1 cup/240ml of dried mushroom steeping liquid
4 tablespoons of buckwheat
2 eggs
2 tablespoons of flour
butter
salt
black pepper

Fry the mushrooms in a saucepan in some oil with the onion for 6 minutes. Put the buckwheat in the pan. Add 1 cup of the water the mushrooms were steeped in. Cover and cook on a low heat for 10 minutes. Add the egg and some salt and pepper and mix.

Stuff the mix into the fish. Place in a baking dish with some butter and cook in a preheated oven at 350F/176C for 40 minutes.

Pork Roast

Ingredients

4 lbs/1.8 kg pork joint
2 chopped onions
4 beetroots
1 lb/453g of prunes (with stone taken out)
1 cup/240ml of sour cream
flour
2 tablespoons of oil
1 teaspoon of paprika
salt

Rub the meat with flour and some salt and pepper.

Put in a saucepan/dutch oven with some oil and cook for 6 minutes - browning all sides. Add the onions and 1 cup/240ml of water. Cover and cook on a low heat for 1 hour.

Pit the beetroot in a saucepan. Cover with water and bring to the boil, then cook on a low heat for 40 minutes - until cooked.

Chop the beetroot and add to to the pan with the meat, along with the prunes and the water the beetroot was cooked in. Cook on a low heat for 7 minutes.

Remove the meat. Put a tablespoon of flour in the pan with the sour cream. Mix and cook on a low heat to make a sauce. Add some salt and pepper and the paprika and stir.

Serve the sauce with the meat.

Goulash (Bograch)

Ingredients

2.2 lbs/1 kg of beef pieces
2 chopped carrots
1 chopped onion
3 chopped potatoes
2 chopped bell peppers
14oz/400g of chopped tomatoes
1 tablespoon of tomato paste/puree
one clove of garlic
1 teaspoon of paprika
1 and two thirds of a cup/400ml of beer
salt
black pepper
dill
oil

Fry the beef in some oil for 6 minutes. Add the onion and carrot and fry for 10 minutes. Add the bell pepper and cook for 6 minutes. Add the beer and cook on a low heat for 1 hour.

Add the garlic, paprika, tomatoes, tomato puree and potato along with some salt and pepper. Stir and cook for 30 minutes.

Add some fresh dill before serving

Pork with Beetroot (Shpundra)

Ingredients

14 oz/400g of bacon
2 chopped beetroot
2 chopped onions
1 cup/240ml of beet kvass
flour
oil
black pepper
lemon juice
dill

Coat the bacon in some flour, salt and pepper. Fry in oil for 10 minutes until browned. Add the onion and fry for 6 minutes. Add the beetroot and cook for 5 minutes.

Add the lemon juice, beet kvass and some salt and pepper. Cover and cook on a low heat for 1 hour.

Add some dill when cooked.

Chicken Pilaf (Plov)

Ingredients

10 oz/290g of chicken cut into pieces
2 chopped carrots
1 chopped onion
black pepper
salt

Cook the meat in some oil in a pan for 6 minutes. Add the carrot and cook for 4 minutes. Add the onion and cook for 5 minutes. Add salt and pepper.

Add the rice, cover it with hot water. Cover and cook on a low heat for 40 minutes - until the rice is cooked

Cutlets (Sichenyky)

Ingredients

1.1 lb/500g of minced/ground beef
3.1 oz/110g of white bread
5 tablespoons of dry breadcrumbs
half a chopped onion
2 grated cloves of garlic
half a cup/120ml of water
half a cup/120ml of milk
2 eggs
1 beaten egg for outside
black pepper
salt

Soak the bread in the water and milk. Add the beef and mix.

Mix the eggs, garlic, onion and some salt and pepper. Add to the beef. Make into burger shapes. Dip in the beaten egg, then in the breadcrumbs.

Fry in a pan for 6 minutes on each side - until cooked and browned.

Stuffed Cabbage (Holubtsi)

Ingredients

5 oz/150g of minced beef
1 cabbage with stalk removed
1 chopped onion
3 cups/525g of cooked rice
salt
pepper
half a cup/120ml of tomato juice

Fry the beef and in a pan with some oil for 7 minutes.

Put the rice, onion, beef and some salt and pepper in a bowl and mix.

Put the cabbage in a pan of boiling water. Cook on a low heat for 8 minutes. Remove the leaves from the cabbage.

Put a bit of the meat mix on each cabbage leaf. Roll the leaf. Put in a baking dish.

Bake in a preheated oven at 350F/176C for 1 and half hours.

Goose with Apple Stuffing

Ingredients

1 goose
1.7 lb/800g of chopped potatoes
4 peeled cored apples cut into slices
4 cored apples
3 tablespoons of white wine
salt
pepper

Rub the goose with wine, salt and pepper, Leave to marinate in the refrigerator for 10 hours.

Put the potatoes in boiling water. Bring to the boil then cook on a low heat for 8 minutes.

Stuff the goose with the apple slices and potato.

Cook in a preheated oven at 356F/180C for 1 and a half hours.

Put the 4 apples in the pan and cook for another hour - until goose is cooked.

Serve goose with stuffing and apples.

Buckwheat with Pork (Kasha)

Ingredients

1 cup/180g of buckwheat
2 cups/480ml of hot water
half a lb/226g of minced pork
1 chopped onion
1 chopped carrot
1 chopped clove of garlic
1 tablespoon of tomato paste/puree
salt
black pepper
oil

Heat some oil in a saucepan. Add the buckwheat and cook for 5 minutes. Put the buckwheat in a separate dish.

Put some more oil in the pan, them coo the onion and carrot for 5 minutes. Add the meat and cook for 10 minutes. Add the garlic and tomato. Add the buckwheat with the water and some salt and pepper.

Cover and cook on a low heat for 15 minutes.

Chicken Kiev
(Kotleta po-kyivsky)

Ingredients

4.9 oz/140g chicken fillet
1.7 oz/50g of dried breadcrumbs
1 tablespoon of chopped dill
2 tablespoons of butter
1 crushed clove of garlic
1 beaten egg
salt
pepper
oil

Beat the chicken fillet. Season with salt and pepper.

Mix the dill, garlic and butter and place on the chicken. Wrap the chicken to ensure there are no gaps. Dip in eggs, then breadcrumbs. Fry in oil in a pan for 6 minutes.

Then place on a baking tray and cook on a medium heat for 15 minutes - until cooked.

Pork Roll with Mushrooms (Kruchenyky)

Ingredients

1.1 lb/500g of pork fillets
1.1 lb/500g of chopped mushrooms
3.5 oz/100g of chopped carrot
3.5 oz/100g of chopped onions
240ml/1 cup of stock
dill
black pepper
salt
oil

Beat the pork fillets, then season with salt and pepper.

Fry the onion and carrot in oil for 5 minutes. Add the mushrooms and cook for 10 minutes.

Put the vegetable mix on the pork slices. Roll the slices up, and tie them up.

Fry the pork in oil for 7 minutes.

Put the pork in a casserole dish. Add the stock. Cook in a medium preheated oven for 50 minutes.

Top with dill before serving.

Meat Patties (Kotlety)

Ingredients

1 lb/453g ground/minced beef
half a cup/50g of cracker crumbs
1 chopped onions
1 chopped clove of garlic
1 egg
1 tablespoon of milk
salt
black pepper
oil

Put all ingredients apart from oil in a bowl. Mix well.

Make into patty shapes. Brown them in the oil n a pan on a
high heat for a few minutes, then fry for 20 minutes, turning
several times, until cooked.

Meat Jelly (Holodets)

Ingredients

1.1 lb/500g of beef
6 teaspoons of gelatine
1 peeled onion
2 bay leaves
salt
pepper
1 carrot

Put the beef, onion, carrot, bay leaves and some salt and pepper in a saucepan. Cover the meat with water. Bring to the boil - remove any foam. Cover and cook on a low heat for 3 and a half hours.

Remove the meat, onion, carrot and bay leaves. Strain the cooking liquid into a jug.

Shred the meat. Put it in a glass dish. Add the gelatine to the cooking liquid and pour into the dish. Place in the refrigerator for 12 hours to set.

Pork and Prunes

Ingredients

2 lb/907g chopped pork
2 chopped onions
3 chopped cloves of garlic
1 cup/225g of prunes with stones taken out
5 black peppercorns
1 bay leaf
1 teaspoon of cinnamon
half a cup/120ml of red wine
half a cup/120ml of beef stock
half a cup/120ml of black tea
butter
oil
salt
black pepper

Put the prunes in a bowl with the tea and leave for 30 minutes.

Put some butter and oil in a pan with the onion and cook for 10 minutes. Put the onions on a plate.

Put the pork in the pan with some oil and butter and cook for 10 minutes - until browned.

Add the onions, wine, stock, peppercorns, cinnamon, bay leaf and some salt and pepper.

Bring to the boil.

Put the mix in a casserole dish, cover and bake in a preheated oven at 350F/176C for 45 minutes.

Add the prunes and garlic. Cook for 25 minutes more. Remove

cover and cook for 10 minutes.

Remove bay leaf and serve.

Cottage Cheese Cake

Honey Cake

Pearl Barley Pudding (Kutia)

Ingredients

1 cup/180 of pearl barley
half a cup/82g of poppy seeds
half a cup/112g of chopped toasted almonds
half a cup/170g of honey
5 chopped dried apricots
half a cup/75g of raisins
1 tablespoon of sugar

Put the pearl barley in a pan. Add about 6 cups/1.4 litres of water, cover and bring the barley to the boil. Then cook on a low heat for 35 minutes - until the barley is cooked. Drain the barley and keep the liquid.

Put the poppy seed in a jug of boiling water and leave for 25 minutes. Drain them then grind in a food processor.

Put the barley in a bowl. Add the barley liquid and the rest of the ingredients and mix. Put the mix into a greased baking dish. Cook in a preheated oven as 325F/162C.

Cool before serving.

Honey Cake (Medovik)

Ingredients

3 tablespoons of honey
2 cups/480ml of milk
3 egg
3 oz/90g of butter
2 cups/360g of flour
1 teaspoon of vanilla extract
2 cups/400g of sugar
1 teaspoon of baking soda

Put the honey, butter and half the sugar in a glass bowl. Place over a pan of boiling water for 6 minutes, stirring all the time. Add the baking soda and mix. Take off the heat and leave for 4 minutes.

Add 2 eggs and stir well. Add 12 oz/340g of flour and mix to make a dough. Put the mix in the freezer for 1 hour.

Make 8 balls from the dough. Pit them in the freezer for 30 minutes.

Roll out each ball and make a circle shape from each dough shape. Keep the waste pastry.

Put the pastry on some baking paper on a tray. Cook in the oven for 5 minutes.

Boil half the milk. Put the rest of the milk in a bowl with the rest of the flour, sugar and an egg. Mix. Then add to the hot milk and stir well. Cook on a low heat for 8 minutes - until thickened. Take off the heat. Add the butter and vanilla and stir.

Layer the pastry circles, putting the icing on top of each piece of pastry. Put the waste pastry on top. Place in the refrigerator for 10 hours.

Cottage Cheese Cake (Babka)

Ingredients

1.1 lb/500g of cottage cheese
half a cup/75g of raisins
1 and a quarter cups/250g of sugar
3 eggs - yolks and white separated
4 tablespoons of biscuit/cookie crumbs
half a cup/100ml of sour cream/smetana
butter
salt
cinnamon

Mix the egg whites with the sugar to make a paste. Add the yolks with the cream and cottage cheese, and stir to make a mix. Add the raisins and cinnamon.

Grease a baking dish with butter. Put a layer of biscuit crumbs in the dish to make a pastry case. Pour in the cheese mix.

Bake in a preheated oven at 356F/180C for 40 minutes.

Easter Cheese (Paska)

Ingredients

15 oz/425g farmer/ricotta cheese
11 oz/311g of cream cheese
half a cup/113g of butter
4 egg yolks
half a cup/100g of sugar
1 teaspoon of vanilla extract
2 teaspoons of lemon juice
1 tablespoon of honey
1 cup/100g of dried fruits

Mix the cheese, butter and eggs on a bowl. Add the vanilla, sugar and lemon juice.

Put a cheesecloth in a sieve. Place the sieve over a bowl. Add the mix to the cheesecloth, then wrap it in the cloth. Put a weight on top, then leave to drain in the refrigerator for 24 hours.

Put the cheese on a bowl. Top with the dried fruit.

Plum and Cheese Dumplings

Ingredients

10 oz/280g of cottage cheese
1 egg yolk
1 teaspoon of lemon zest
1 tablespoon of currants
1 tablespoon of sugar
5 chopped plums
half a cup/100g of sugar
sour cream
oil

dumpling dough

2 cups/240g of flour
6 oz/170g of butter
1 and a half tablespoons of sour cream
1 egg

Mix the cheese, egg yolk and sugar and make a paste. Add the currants and zest.

Mix the dough ingredients to make the dough. Place in the refrigerator for 40 minutes.

Roll out the dough. Cut into biscuit/cookie sized shapes. Put some of the cheese mix on half the dough shapes. Fold them and seal the cheese inside. On the other half of the dough shapes put plums and some sugar. Fold these again to encase the plum mix.

Put the dumplings in a pan of boiling water and cook for 3 minutes. Drain.

Put some oil in a pan. Add the dumplings and cook them for 5 minutes - browning on each side.

Serve with sour cream.

Apple Cake (Yabluchnyk)

Ingredients

1 and a half/170g cups of flour
quarter of a cup/50g of sugar
2 teaspoons of baking powder
half a cup/113g of butter
third of a cup/80ml of cream
4 peeled cored and sliced apples
half a teaspoon of salt

topping

2 tablespoons of butter
half a cup/110g of brown sugar
2 tablespoons of flour
1 teaspoon of cinnamon

Mix the flour, salt, sugar, and baking powder in a bowl. Mix in the butter. Add the egg and cream. Stir to make a dough. Put the dough into a greased baking tray.

Put the apples in the pastry in layers. Mix the topping ingredients and sprinkle over the top.

Cook in a preheated oven at 375F/190C for 25 minutes.

Strawberry Jam

Ingredients

1 lb/453g of strawberries
12 oz/340g of sugar

Put the strawberries and sugar in a saucepan. Cook on a low
heat for 20 minutes stirring several times. Bring to the boil,
then cook on a low heat for 1 hour, again stirring occasionally.

Cheese Pancakes (Syrniki)

Ingredients

9 oz/250g of farmers cheese (or cottage cheese)
1 egg
3 tablespoons of caster/superfine sugar
4 tablespoons of flour
salt
oil

Mix the egg and sugar to make a paste. Stir in the flour, cheese, sugar and some salt. Make a dough.

Form into biscuit/cookie shapes. Fry on a medium heat for 5 minutes on each side.

Serve with jam.

Walnut Stuffed Prunes

Ingredients

walnuts
prunes with stones taken out
whipping cream
sugar
chocolate
cream

Toast some walnuts by cooking them in a frying pan for 6 minutes.

Mix some whipping cream with sugar cream. Put walnut in each prune and put some cream in the prune. Put the prunes in a bowl. Add some cream and sprinkle grated chocolate and crushed walnuts.

Coffee Jelly

Ingredients

10 oz/300g of coffee
5 tablespoons of dried gelatine (or 2 oz/50g of gelatine sheets)
1 cup/200g of sugar
1 cup/240ml of cream

Put the gelatine in a glass of water to soften.

Mix hot coffee, sugar, cream and the gelatine.

Strain the liquid into a bowl using a sieve.

Place in a mould and refrigerate until set.

Plum Kyselitsa

Ingredients

14 oz/400g of plums
2 thirds of a cup/135g of sugar
2 tablespoons of cornflour
4 cups/960ml of water

Boil the plums in the water for 10 minutes. Rub them through a sieve and keep the liquid.

Put the plum juice in a saucepan. Bring to the boil then add the corn flour and sugar. Cook on a medium heat for 10 minutes.

Serve the drink hot.

Uzvar

Ingredients

7 oz/210g of dried apple
3 oz/80g of raisins
10 oz/280g of dried pears
2 quarters of a cup/260g of honey
4 pints/2 litres of water

Put the fruit in water for 12 minutes.

Put the fruit in a pan of boiling water. Cook on a medium heat for 30 minutes. Add the honey and bring to the boil.

Serve the drink hot or cold.

Spiced Vodka

Ingredients

2 peppercorns
1 stick of cinnamon
1 tablespoon of sugar
1 tablespoon of lemon zest
2 tablespoons of honey
2 cups/475ml of vodka
1 cup/240ml of water

Put half the water in a pan with the zest, peppercorns and cinnamon. Cook on a low heat for 12 minutes. Strain the liquid into a bowl.

Put the rest of the water, honey and sugar into a bowl. Bring to the boil. Add the other liquid and the vodka. Cook a low heat for 6 minutes.

Kvass

Ingredients

1.3 lb/630g/ of breadcrumbs from rye bread
5 teaspoons of yeast
1 lb/430g of sugar
2 teaspoons of flour
lemon slices
12 pints/6 litres of hot water

Put the breadcrumbs in a bowl. Add hot water. Leave for 6 hours. Add the flour and half the yeast to the bread mix. Leave for 1 hour.

Drain the bread mix and keep the liquid. Add the sugar and the rest of the yeast to the liquid, then leave for 10 hours - in a warm place.

Drain the liquid through a sieve. Put the liquid in bottles with lemon slices. Leave in the refrigerator for 2 hours.